Fashion Graphics

Patrick John Ireland

B.T. Batsford Ltd., London

First published 1997
© Patrick John Ireland 1997

Printed in Hong Kong
for the Publisher
B.T. Batsford Ltd
583 Fulham Road
London SW6 5BY
http://www.batsford.com

A CIP catalogue is available for this book is available from the British Library.

ISBN 0 7134 7418 1 741 · 672 IRE (050)

Acknowledgements

I would like to thank the following for their help in the preparation of *Fashion Graphics*: Peter Dawson, Vice Principal, Dean of the Faculty of Constructed Design, Bournemouth College of Art and Design; all the Lecturers at the School of Fashion at Bournemouth for their encouragement; Christina Barry, Jacky Jeans and Teresa Coburn for their advice and support; the students who allowed me to show examples of their work; James Philip, the College's in-house photographer for the photographs of students and their work; Val Fisher, Programme Director of the BA Costume for Screen and Stage; costume designer Stephen West; Richard Reynolds and Martina Stansbie at B.T. Batsford Ltd.; Katrina Dallamore and Craig Hadley at DW Design; Rainer Usselmann for the photograph on p4; Word Processing Services, Marlow, Bucks. for advice on the use of the photocopier; Tim Harvey of a boville wright Ltd, Maidenhead for advice on artist's materials.

Contents

Introduction

The purpose of this book is to encourage you to experiment with different art materials and to develop your fashion graphic presentation techniques. I have illustrated and described effects that can be achieved with various media and presentation techniques although it must be stressed that there are no rules and you should explore for yourself the many that are available.

Fashion illustration techniques are often highly individual to a particular artist. As a student you will discover methods and effects almost by accident. The aim of *Fashion Graphics* is to encourage you to move beyond the basics and develop a personal approach to fashion illustration, layout and presentation.

It is important to be aware of the different areas of fashion drawing and the illustrative skills that best suit the purpose of the sketch. Some of these areas will be explored in this introduction.

Student working in a studio.

Fashion Illustrators

Students of fashion who are
interested in developing their
design drawing and illustration
skills should make a study of the
work of fashion illustrators of the
past. Look at techniques and
styles and also for the influences
of both contemporary and classic
fine artists. Fashion illustrators
were often inspired by the work of
fine artists, in particular that of
Braque, Toulouse-Lautrec,
Mondrian, Matisse, Gauguin,
Kandinsky and Picasso, and have
explored the graphic decorative
possibilities that were to be found
in these artists's work.

Fashion artists from the 1900s to study include Paul Iribe, Erté, Georges
Lepape and Benito, many of whom started their careers with *La Gazette
du Bon Ton*, the French fashion journal. This was a golden period for
fashion magazines and for fashion illustration. The 1920s saw *Vogue* and
Harper's Bazaar firmly established as the leading fashion magazines. These
magazines have subsequently promoted artists Christian Bérart, Eric (Carl
Erickson), Willaumee (signed RBW), Tod Draz, John Ward, Francis
Marshall, Robb, Stemp, Antonio and Colin Barnes, amongst many others.

1 Quick design sketches produced by
  a very fine pen with a watercolour
  wash.

2 Faces and hands are only
  suggested.

3 Note the exaggeration of the legs
  to emphasize the image.

Fashion Design Sketching

Designers use fashion drawing as a way of expressing their ideas on paper when working on a collection. The finished garment design may well change from the initial drawing but the sketch is the starting point of the designer's ideas. Developing these ideas and working on the design theme is an important stage in the design process. The drawings should be clear, including details of the silhouette and how the garment would be cut, and indicating the shape of pockets, placement of seams and type of sleeve and fastenings. The sketch should reflect a feeling for the fabric and a strong sense of fashion and style. Students of fashion rely on their design drawings both to get a job and to sell their designs so the ability to make quick, stylish design sketches is vital.

This style of sketching is often referred to as 'designer's handwriting'. The sketches are stylized, suggesting the figure, hands, head and feet with a few lines only. Despite their brevity, the sketches should still project a fashion image. The colours, patterns and textures are represented by pencils, markers or watercolour and the back view is either indicated as a flat diagrammatic sketch or on a figure. Explanatory notes should be added when necessary and samples of suggested fabrics attached.

Presentation Drawings

A collection of design sketches for an assessment, interview or for selling your work to a client requires a more finished drawing style. The presentation of the work is extremely important. The sketches should project the fashion image and fabrics, colours, patterns and textures should be clearly represented. Always select a figure pose that reflects the mood of the design.

Lorenzo Iriate (ND2, Bournemouth College of Art and Design)

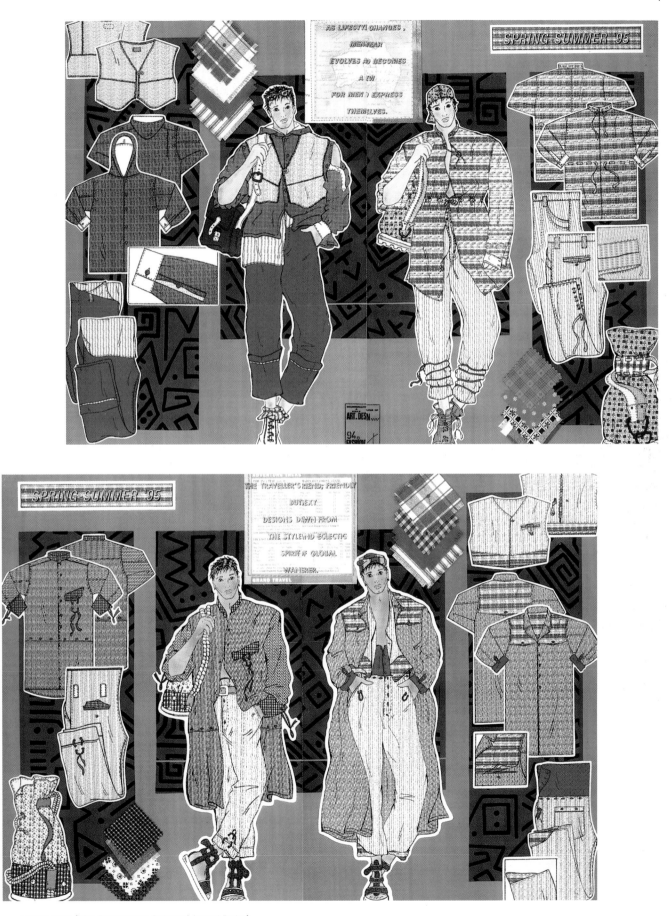

Lorenzo Iriate (ND2, Bournemouth College of Art and Design)

Competitions

Students have the opportunity to enter competitions sponsored by clothing and textile companies that cover many different areas of fashion, from day and eveningwear to sportswear and more specialized areas. Good presentation of the designs is crucial. The format of the work will usually be determined by the rules of the competition.

Storyboards

These boards are used professionally when giving a presentation to clients or for display on exhibition stands. Storyboards may also be used in retail stores to inform staff of the new trends and colours that will be promoted throughout the store during the coming season. They are often photographed for fashion and textile magazines and prediction books where they are combined with articles promoting and predicting fashion trends and influences.

Suzzanna Barnes (Bournemouth College of Art and Design)

Fashion students should produce storyboards when working on a collection of design ideas. The boards illustrate mood, colours and the inspirational research undertaken in answer to a design brief. A pinboard may be used to display reference materials, sketches and fabrics when working on a collection of design ideas.

Maxine Etheridge (Bournemouth College of Art and Design)

Andrew Piggins
(Hastings College of Art and Technology)

Visual Studies

For visual studies projects, students are set a brief which aims to develop visual awareness and encourage understanding of the three-dimensional construction of objects. These objects are used as the basis for experiments in line, texture, colour and form, with students using a selection of media and illustration and presentation techniques.

For the examples illustrated, the project was entitled 'Eco Art to Fashion', with natural objects used as the starting point.

Charlotte Chamier (ND1, Bournemouth College of Art and Design)

Vera Macedo (ND2, Bournemouth College of Art and Design)

Fashion Journalism

Fashion editorials in
newspapers and magazines
are illustrated with fashion
sketches and photographs.
A drawing may convey
information more accurately
than a photograph as, on
black and white newsprint,
line work has more impact
than the grey tones of a
photograph. The artist can
represent a particular
fashion image with economy
of line, emphasizing specific
features of a designer's
collection: the silhouette,
collar or sleeves.

An illustrator is employed
for their particular style.
Although this style may
exaggerate design features
to project a certain image,
the illustration should not
distort the design and
should clearly convey the
general feel of a collection.

1 Fashion illustrations in watercolour wash
  on Bockingford textured watercolour paper.
2 Left to right: watercolour effects: wash;
  sharp edge; dry brush; wet into wet.

Fashion Forecasting

Fashion forecasting agencies predict fashion trends in womenswear, menswear and childrenswear, providing information for major manufacturers, retailers, high street stores, and, when requested, for individual clients. As made-up garments will not yet be available, a fashion illustration is the most effective way to convey this information. The agencies employ designers and illustrators both full time and as freelances. Their predictions cover fashion design themes and influences, styles, fabrics and colours, and they work often up to 20 months in advance of the retail business. Agencies also make use of specialist researchers and market analysts to promote the future trends in fashion to their customers.

As part of their research, illustrators for agencies may travel abroad to collect ideas and information for their presentation, working closely with the manufacturers of cosmetics, accessories and textiles. The work is very precise, requiring diagrammatic drawings that use different line values. The proportions of the garments must be accurate in every detail and relate to the basic proportions of the figure. The drawings have to be clear so that they are easy for a manufacturer or store buyer to read. The presentation is of a high standard and includes fashion illustrations represented on figures, diagrammatic drawings, sample fabrics, colour charts and promotional material on inspirations and fashion styles.

Equipment: Working on the Light Box

The light box is a bright light in a box with a glass surface. The illustration is placed on the glass with drawing paper over it. The illustration is illuminated, so that you can see it through the paper on which you are working. The light box allows you to develop a final drawing from a rough sketch.

Equipment: Working on the Computer

Working on the computer enables you to experiment with colour, line values, layout and lettering. Once the image has been scanned, you can try out different effects very quickly before making your final decision and printing the illustration out.

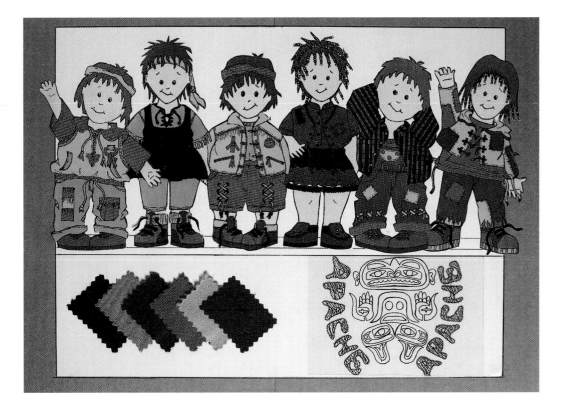

1 Presentation boards produced on the computer by Maxine Etheridge, Bournemouth College of Art and Design.

Figure Drawing

Figure Proportions

The design sketch is essential to expressing your design ideas. It is important to develop your drawing skills so you can sketch figures and garments with speed. Your figure drawing will be much improved if you practise drawing from a model or attend life classes and study anatomy.

When sketching the figure, always refer to the basic figure proportions. The height of the average figure varies from between seven-and-a-half to eight times the height of the head. Check the balance of the figure by noting the line from the pit of the neck to the foot that is taking the weight of the body. The centre front line will be helpful for balancing the design details.

When fashion illustration is used for advertising or promotion work, the figures
are often distorted to emphasize current fashion trends. Legs are elongated,
shoulders enlarged, waist and hips stressed, and details either exaggerated or
simplified for effect. However, a design sketch or a design presentation drawing
is usually presented on a figure with less exaggerated proportions.

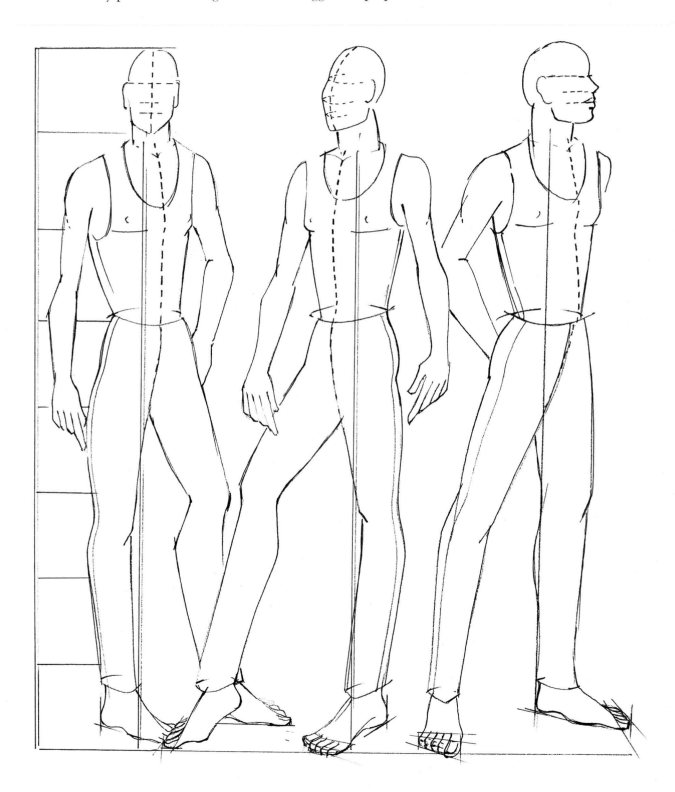

Stylized Figures

The figures in these presentation boards have been stylized to project
the mood of the design. Legs are elongated and shoes
enlarged to emphasize the image desired.

Maxine Etheridge

(Bournemouth College of Art and Design)

Maxine Etheri

(Bournemouth College of Art and Des

Marilyn Edwards (Bournemouth College of Art and Design)

Maria Fernandez (Bournemouth College of Art and Design)

Figure Templates

Produce a variety of poses to use as figure templates, always working to the correct figure proportions.

1 Figure templates developed from life drawings.

2 Fashion sketches are developed from the figure templates.

3 The line drawings are combined with textural effects.

Using Templates

If you have difficulty drawing the figure, templates are helpful when design ideas have to be developed quickly.

- Sketch a template or photocopy one from this book.
- Place the template under a sheet of semi-transparent paper or on a light box, which enables you to use paper of different thicknesses.
- Develop sketches over the figure in a free style.
- Remove and complete the sketch.
- Look at figure reference books for ideas for new poses when a model is not available. These books encorporate a wide range of poses viewed from different angles.

- Create templates working from a model or from a photograph.
- Study anatomy and life drawing.
- Develop poses working from the imagination when you have confidence in your life drawing.
- Experiment with more stylized figures once you can draw the figure proportions of men, women and children with confidence.

Drawing from the Model

In fashion drawing, the pose of the model should convey a mood reflecting the occasion and environment in which the design would be worn. Work from life or from photographs to develop a range of suitable poses.

1 Line sketches are developed from life with a Pentel pen, the poses reflecting the style of the garments.
2 The sketches are enlarged on the photocopier and copied on to tinted pastel paper.
3 Soft pastels are applied to the sketches, with the tinted paper treated as a mid-tone.
4 Fixative spray is added to the illustrations to prevent smearing.

Pastels

The tip of the pastel stick is good for fine work and the side will create broad lines. A fixative spray should always be used to avoid smearing while you are working. Fixative is also useful for isolating areas of the design so that you can work on specific sections. Many papers are specially made for pastel work.

- Vary pastel tones by altering the pressure on the stick as you work.
- Blend colours either with a stump or with your fingers.
- Mix strokes, dots and dashes to represent the effects of textures.
- Treat tinted papers as a mid-tone and add another dimension to your work.

Sketching from Life

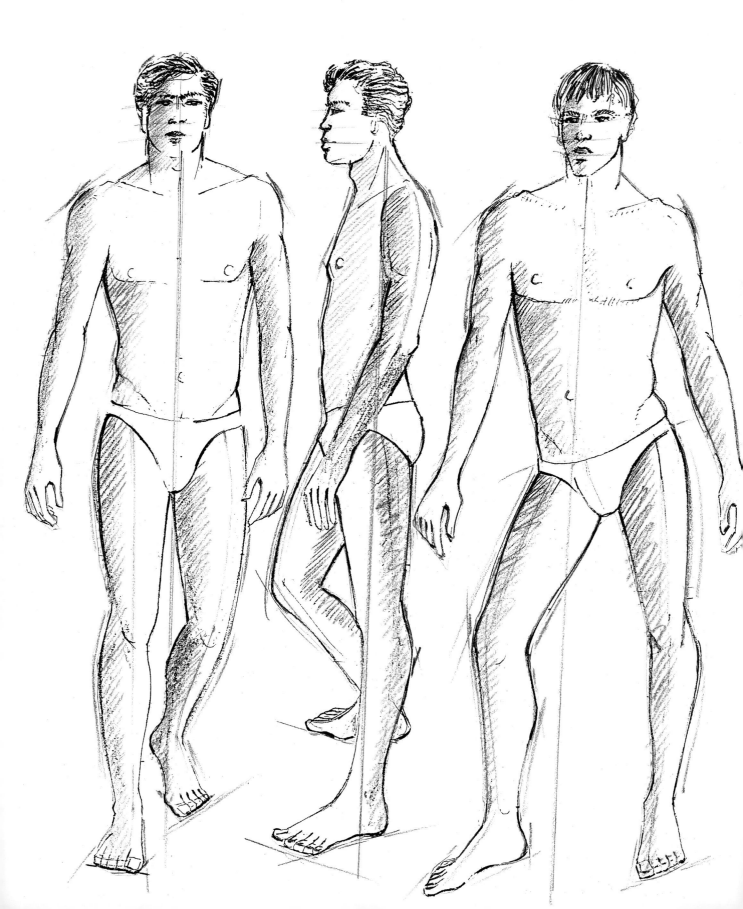

1 Left: Figure poses are developed from sketches from life.
2 The figures are outlined in pen and ink with soft pencil used for
   the tone.
3 Above: Fashion sketches illustrating casualwear are developed from
   these life sketches using a soft black Stabilo pencil with a soft black
   pastel for the shading.

Oil Pastels

The thick texture of oil pastels gives strong solid areas of clear, brilliant colour. Oil pastels are not suited to small-scale detailed work as the sticks are too large. Pastel papers are the best surface to work on.

- Experiment with colour by blending the pastels.
- Use as dry colour or try wet with turpentine or solvent spray to blend the colours.
- Practise representing textures by leaving some areas white to represent highlights of the fabric. This will prevent the drawing from appearing too dense.
- Make the texture or tone of the paper a feature of the fashion illustration.
- Always apply a fixative to your work to prevent it smearing.

1 Left: Fashion illustration in oil pastels on a textured paper. The stylized figure is drawn from the imagination, working to the basic proportions.
2 Areas of white are left to suggest the texture of the suede jacket.
3 The cord of the trousers is created by scratching into the oil pastels with a sharp pencil.
4 Note the selection of the pose to reflect the style of the garment.

Gouache

Gouache is similar to watercolour, but is mixed with white pigment and extender to make it opaque. It provides flat, solid areas of colour and is good for strong contrasts of tone and colour.

• For a more free technique, apply gouache with water so that the brush strokes are visible. This will give a translucent effect.

1 Fashion illustration using gouache.

2 A thick Pentel pen is used to outline the figures.

3 Areas of white are left to suggest the design detail of seams and pockets.

4 To represent the textures of the shirts, gouache is blended with water, leaving visible brush strokes.

5 Note the stylized pose to emphasize the mood of the design.

1 Line drawing with a fine Pilot Hi
  Techpoint pen illustrating stylized
  poses that have been worked up
  from the basic proportions.

Illustrating Children's Clothes

When illustrating children's clothes, it is important to be aware that the proportions of children change as they grow. Initially, you might find it helpful to work from the basic proportions illustrated opposite.

Whenever possible, sketch from life, observing children's attitudes and the way in which they move, walk, skip and run. It is difficult to draw children in a set pose as they are not patient models. It is better to make quick sketches from life and then develop them.

Experiment with different styles of design illustration, from realistic representations to a more stylized approach.

Use of the Camera

Photographs are useful for capturing poses which you can later develop for illustration.

- Collect a series of photographs to use as background effects.
- Practise enlarging your photographs on the photocopier.

1 yrs   2 yrs   4 yrs   6 yrs   8 yrs   10 yrs

12 yrs   15 yrs

Pencils

Schwan Carothello Pencils

These smooth, coloured pencils give intense even areas of colour without streaking. They can be used dry or with solvent.

- Experiment combining these pencils with turpentine or solvent spray, blending colours with a brush or cotton wool bud.
- Try blending colours by applying layers on top of one another.

1 Left: Firstly, the figures are drawn in line with a black pen.

2 Colours are applied dry in some areas of the illustration and blended in combination with solvent spray in others.

3 A cotton wool bud is used to blend the solvent and pencils on the jacket.

4 Pencil is used to pick out details such as the edging of the cape.

5 Soft black pencil shaded over the surface of the garments gives the effect of blanket cloth.

6 Areas of white are left to highlight the folds.

7 Presentation: The figures are cut out and mounted against a white presentation board for contrast and a sharp finish.

Schwan Stabilo Pencils

Black-and-white tonal drawings can have as much impact as a full-colour illustration. Newspapers and magazines often require fashion drawings in black and white and you should develop your skill in producing drawings with various line and tonal values.

- Sharpen the point of the pencils to represent the details of the sketch.
- Experiment with applying different pressures on the pencil to achieve variation in intensities of tone.
- Shade from light to dark.
- Try working on a large scale to encourage a free technique.

1 Right: Poses are developed very quickly from models on the catwalk.
2 Pastel powder is applied and blended on the cheeks with a cotton wool bud.

1 Heads sketched from a model in pen and ink, working with a free technique.
2 The sketches are developed with soft black pencils.
3 Note the effect of using different pressures on the intensity of tone.

1 Above: Free stylized sketch with a Pentel fine line pen on heavy textured cartridge paper.

2 Colours are then applied lightly to the sketch.

3 For the textures of the garments, black pencil creates the thickness of cord; trousers, waistcoat and bag are shaded with black lead pencil to emphasize tone and texture and the patterns of the knitted waistcoat are worked up with short strokes of Derwent fine art colour pencils.

4 Presentation: The figure is cut out and placed against a panel of colours reflecting the colours of the design. To offset the figure, the complete panel is spraymounted on to a white card for a sharp contrast.

Observation Drawings

Select garments and accessories to sketch in detail. Try sketching shoes from different angles noting their construction, shape and proportions. Look at their decorative effects, the type of material used, the thickness of the sole and the shape of the heel. Use a variety of styles to sketch from and experiment with different media and paper textures.

Charcoal Pencils

The charcoal pencil is very adaptable for shading and for reproducing textures. Different effects may be achieved by working with a selection of pencil thicknesses and paper textures.

- Use cotton wool buds for shading and creating lighter areas.
- Sharpen the pencils when embarking on more detailed work.
- Always use a good fixative when working with charcoal pencils.

1 Sketches produced on a textured cartridge paper, with a fine black pen to note the details.

2 Shading is in charcoal pencil, leaving light areas to emphasize the style features.

1 The outline of the shoe is sketched using a fine black pen on textured cartridge paper.

2 The shoe is then shaded in a free style with charcoal pencils.

3 Note the areas of white left on the laces and piping to emphasize these details.

Water Soluble Pens

When water is brushed over water soluble pens, the colour will dissolve into a wash tone. The more colour you have used in your sketch the stronger and darker the tone will be. This technique requires patience.

- Keep a paper towel to hand to blot the areas that are too dark.
- Experiment with the medium before applying colour to your drawing.
- Always use a waterproof ink to outline your drawings when using water soluble pens.

1 The figures are sketched in a black waterproof ink on textured cartridge paper.

2 Water soluble pens are used to colour the sketches.

3 To add tonal contrast and provide a wash effect on the trousers, water is applied over the coloured areas.

Aquarella Sticks

These sticks combine the advantages of colour pencils, oil-based pastels, crayons and classical watercolours in a single product. Use them just like watercolour, working up the paint straight from the stick. The high pigment content means that the brush rapidly absorbs the colour. The sticks may be purchased in boxes or as single sticks. Like pastels the sticks leave a waxy mark of intense colour which can be blended with other colours or worked into extended areas of uniform colour.

- Try applying Aquarella sticks dry to the paper and working over the drawing with a wet paintbrush.
- Experiment with papers of different colours and textures.

1 The background is represented as a water wash.
2 The sticks are used with water on the trousers and jumper, and the areas gone over with a dry stick to represent the textures.

Selecting Papers

The paper you use will always influence the effect of your media and the mood of your illustration.

- Dark subdued papers can produce an added brilliance to the effects.
- A hard white paper gives a light delicate effect to your illustration.
- Grained papers are suitable when illustrating textures.

1 Drawings produced with a Rotring propelling pencil with a fine line value on a smooth white Bristol board.

Lead Pencils

The pencil line is influenced by the grade of pencil, the pressure applied, the type of paper and the texture of the paper's surface. Start by making random marks on the paper and discover the potential of the medium.

- Use soft pencils when working on large, quick and bold drawings, hard pencils for more detailed drawings.
- Experiment with different line values before working on your final drawing.

Karisma Graphite Aquarella Pencils

The leads of these pencils have been specially formulated to be soluble in water.

- Try applying a wet brush over areas of the drawing to achieve a dark wash effect.
- Experiment with the effect when working into the tone with a dry pencil.
- Leave areas of white to highlight parts of your illustration.

1 To represent the textures of knitwear, tweed and ribbing, the pencils are used with a wash and the area then worked into with a dry pencil.

Blending Colour Pencils

Schwan Stabilo softcolour pencils, fibre pens and markers can be blended with solvent spray to achieve a variety of effects. Spray the solvent on to the areas of colour and blend the two together.

- Experiment with the different effects produced by blending either with a cotton wool bud or with a paint brush.

1 For these drawings, black pen in outline is combined with Stabilo softcolour pencils.
2 The colours are blended with Stabilo solvent spray and a cotton wool bud.
3 Areas of white are left to suggest the highlights on the surface of the quilted sheen jackets.
4 For contrast, parts of the figures are shaded with a soft 3B pencil.
5 Presentation: The figures are cut out leaving an area of white round them and then spraymounted against colour panels.

Marker Pens

A large selection of marker pens are available which vary in the size and shape of the nib. Marker tips come in four basic shapes: fine, bullet, wedge and brush. Some marker pens have interchangable tips providing a choice of line values. The wedge tip is the most useful shape to work with as it allows you to draw lines of varied widths depending on how you hold the marker pen. Always keep your markers organized in colour tone grouping as this will make it easier when making the transition from one tone to another.

- Experiment with half tones, starting with the lightest colour and working up increasingly darker tones from the same colour range.
- Build up layers of colour.

1 Freeline figure sketches in line, with pale grey marker pen adding strength of tone to the drawings.

Studio Marker Pens

These are available in a wide range of colours and tones.

- Lay colours over one another: they will not dissolve into each other.
- Use these markers to block in flat areas of consistent colour or tone very quickly.

Dry Marker Pens

- Always replace their caps as they tend to dry out very quickly.

Blender Marker Pens

These markers contain pure solvent and are colourless. They can thin, lighten or even remove colour.

- Place tissue paper under the paper you are working on, apply the blender to the coloured area you wish to remove and the colour will come out on to the tissue paper from the back of the art work.

Airbrush Effects

Simple airbrush effects may be achieved with marker pens. Some manufacturers produce an airbrush in conjunction with their markers and a can of airbrush propellant. Marker airbrushes are easy to use as you do not have to mix paint or fill the container. The disadvantage lies in not being able to mix a particular colour and in a limitation of the techniques and effects possible.

Presentation Techniques

- Use photographs to provide suitable background material, suggesting the mood and atmosphere of your design.
- Try enlarging photographs on the photocopier in either black and white or colour for effective background effects.

1 The initial sketch is produced with a soft 3B pencil.

2 The rough sketch is developed as a line drawing by placing it on the glass of a light box, overlaying it with a selected paper and working over it to produce a simple, clean figure outline.

3 Marker pens, softcolour Stabilo pencils used with solvent spray and textured effects complete the illustration.

4 Presentation: The figure is cut out, leaving an irregular margin around it. It is then spraymounted against a coloured panel and photograph. An airbrush is used around one side of the figure.

Marker Pens and Pencils

Marker pens and pencils are most effective when combined together. The markers provide a strong bold statement which is complemented by the fine detail of the pencils.

1 Stylized sketch in a black marker pen with a strong line value.
2 Grey Pantone marker pens are used for the tones of suit and overcoat.
3 The tweed texture is created with a soft grey pencil. Details of face, hat, hands, shoes, shirt and tie are then all added in pencil.
4 Presentation: The figure is cut out and placed against an airbrush background with a section of a photograph as a panel in the background to suggest the mood.

1 These sketches are produced with a fine pen.

2 Faces and figures are shaded with a soft grey pastel powder applied with a cotton wool bud.

3 White pastel is used for highlights on hair, face and dresses.

4 Presentation: The figures are placed against a soft grey airbrush background.

• Use black markers in a free style to suggest the flow, drape and gathers of fabrics.

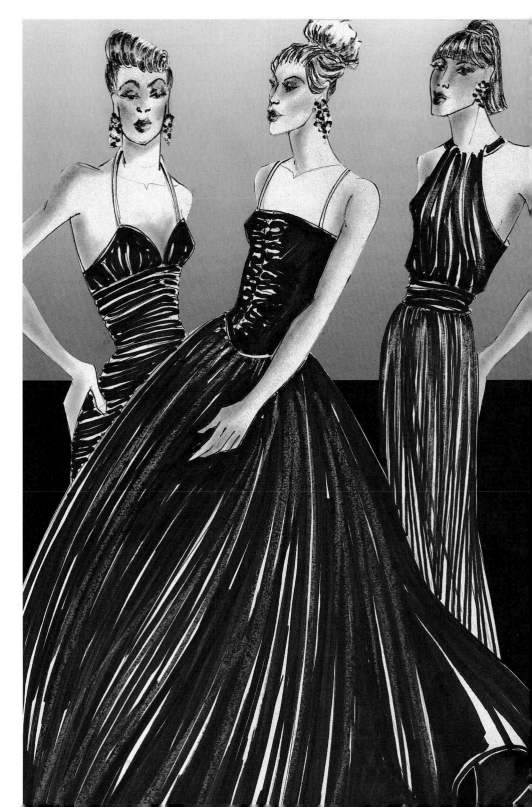

1 This figure is developed in two stages.

2 First, the figure is outlined with a fine point pen.

3 The garment is coloured with Pantone marker pen.

4 The effect of the material is added to the garment by placing a texture under the paper and rubbing over it with a colour pencil.

5 Face and body areas are shaded with soft pastel applied with a cotton wool bud.

6 The hair is developed with a very fine point drawing pen.

1 The figures are sketched with a
   fine line Pilot v ball pen on Bristol
   board.
2 Pantone marker pens are used to
   add colour.
3 Presentation: The figures are cut
   out and mounted against a
   coloured panel and photograph to
   suggest the mood and atmosphere
   appropriate to the garments.

Line and Tone

Working with a marker pen and wash is most effective. The combination of crisply drawn lines and fluid washes creates a very attractive visual appeal, capturing the essence of a design with economy and restraint. Quill pens and reed pens produce very expressive lines which vary according to the amount of pressure applied to the pen. Technical pens produce a line of even thickness which is more suited to a controlled style of drawing.

- Experiment with a range of pens and brushes to discover which are best suited to your purpose.
- When adding tone, keep it simple and clean; it is very easy to overwork the sketch.
- Note how a tone will add solidity to your sketch.

1 These drawings each contain different line values produced with a selection of pens.
2 A pale grey Pantone marker pen is lightly applied where shadows fall to suggest tone.

Drawing in two stages.

1 The initial line drawing is in fine black pen.

2 The completed sketch, with different line values combined with solid black pen, and a pale grey marker highlighting the patterns and textures of the garments.

3 A pale grey Pantone marker pen is used to suggest tone.

Drawing in Reverse

Marker pens will bleed through a sheet of paper to form an image on the reverse side. This can be developed as a deliberate technique and produces very attractive effects. Drawing in reverse requires practice and experimentation.

1 Below: The drawing is produced in pencil on very thin layout paper.
2 Marker pens are applied to the line drawing.
3 The paper is reversed and the illustration developed by sketching into the impression of colour that has bled through, giving a free and fragmented effect.

Mixed Media

The use of one medium is often enough to express what you wish to show in your design illustration. However, you may find it effective to combine paints, pencils, wax crayons and other media in the one drawing.

- Try experimenting on all kinds of papers, considering their texture, colour and weight.
- Familiarize yourself with the marks different media make. Discover how they mix and react to the surface of various papers.

The following are some of the many tools that can be used when working in mixed media

crayons	*conte*
water soluble crayons	*acrylic paints*
wax crayons	*oil pastels*
coloured pencils	*dry pastels*
charcoal pencils	*gouache*
lead pencils	*drawing inks*
coloured felt pens	*indian inks*
water soluble pens	*watercolour and aquarella sticks*
brush marker pens	*chalks*
coloured felt marker pens	*graphite sticks*
ballpoint pens	*solvent spray*
dip nib pens	*fixative*
drawing pens	*selection of papers for collage work*

1 Above: The outline is sketched with a black Pentel pen.
2 The shirt is represented in watercolour, with pen and ink for the pattern.
3 The texture of the trousers is created by working over the illustration with thick black pencil.

1 Right: Fashion illustration demonstrating textured techniques combined with pens, pencils and pastels of differing line values.

1 Mixed media illustrations on tinted pastel papers using collage effects.

2 Sketch the figures in a free style with a fine drawing pen.

3 Colour tones are added with soft pastels and a cotton wool bud.

4 Patterned fabrics are photocopied and reduced to the scale of the
   figures. Garment shapes are traced, cut out and applied to the figures,
   leaving areas of white for seams and design details.

5 Right: Presentation: The figure is cut out and placed against a coloured
   panel and photograph to complement the mood of the garments.

Line Drawings

A well drawn fashion sketch in line can convey a lot of information as well as be an attractive illustration. Line drawings reproduce well and a selection of effects may be produced using different line values and a style that can either be controlled or free.

Textured Effects

- Experiment developing a textured line on a textured paper. The line will break up as the pen moves over the surface of the paper.
- Place a texture under the paper and try sketching over the the paper's surface.
- Use a variety of pens and develop line values, patterns and textures.

Inks

- To overlap washes without dissolving the drawn lines, choose indian ink, which is waterproof.
- For greater flexibility and the ability to blend the lines select a soluble ink or soluble drawing pens.

1 Fine pointed pen for tweed effects.
2 Decorative line values.
3 Pentel Sign Pen with broader tip for the irregular outline round the figure.
4 Areas of solid black were used to complete the effects.
5 The sketch was produced on a smooth surface Bristol board.

1 The figure is outlined with a sketchy free line on a smooth Bristol board.
2 Fine pointed drawing pen for fine lines and dots provides the effect of tweed.
3 A watercolour wash is applied over the sketch.

The range of pens used for line drawing may be divided into five groups: technical pens, plastic-tipped pens, fibre-tipped pens, roller pens and ballpoint pens. New pens are constantly being produced. Always experiment with a pen to see if it produces the line value you require.

• Work on different surfaces of paper, from rough to smooth.
• Try brushing water over a line produced with a soluble ink pen.
• Combine the use of a number of pens in an illustration, producing a variety of line values.

1 Free sketch produced with a soft black drawing pencil.

2 The sketch is then retraced using a light box to achieve a simple line drawing with a pencil.

3 The material of the garments is suggested by placing textures under the paper and rubbing over the illustration.

4 Stabilo softcolour pencils are used to colour the illustration.

5 Fine marker pen highlights the bags, boots and gloves.

6 A Pilot Hi Tecpoint pen is used to pick out the fine details of seaming.

7 Presentation: The figures are cut out leaving an area of white round them and then placed against a contrasting coloured sheet of card for emphasis.

Textures and Patterns

A textured effect is achieved by placing material under the paper, then applying charcoal, crayon or pencil over the surface. It is often more effective to suggest the pattern of texture rather than overworking an illustration. Work from one side of the figure, leaving areas of light to add an extra dimension to your sketch.

- Study the patterns, weaves and textures of fabric.
- Note the behaviour of materials: the way in which they drape and fall into folds.
- Experiment with different media and various paper textures.

1 Fashion illustration in charcoals, pencils and pastel.
2 Experiment with pencils to achieve the effects of tweed before working on the final illustration.

1 Right: Figures were drawn using soft black Stabilo pencils, working on a textured paper.
2 Light textures were added to the figures, taking care not to overwork the illustration.
3 The figures were cut out and arranged on the board so that they overlapped in order to complement the designs.

1 Left: Marker pens are used on the face, hands and trousers.

2 The textured effect on the shirt is achieved by placing a suitable cloth under the paper and applying pencil to the surface.

3 The jacket texture is represented by solvent-based coloured pencils washed with water. A series of short lines make the tweed effect.

4 A soft black Stabilo pencil is used to shade the folds of the jacket.

5 The figure is outlined in black felt tip pen which is also used to emphasize the details.

1 Right: The initial line drawing is produced freely with a pen on an A4 sheet of layout paper.

2 Canvas, embossed paper and hessian are placed under the paper and a black pencil is applied over the surface, creating a variety of textured effects.

3 The illustration was photocopied and enlarged on to to a sheet of A3 marker paper. This paper will not bleed when used with marker pens.

4 Colours were applied with Pantone marker pens in a free style.

5 Areas of white were left to give spontaneity to the figure pose.

6 Presentation: The illustration was cut out and mounted against panels of a photograph and a coloured airbrush background.

• Collect a folder of interesting textured pieces for use when illustrating.

• Attach your textured pieces to thick card to give a firmer surface on which to work.

• Combine a number of textures for a greater effect, but remember to select a thin paper so that the textured impressions will be clearly defined.

• Photocopy your work after you have applied the textures for a clear effect.

• Experiment with photocopying your drawing on to paper of different textures and colours.

• Work over the photocopy with different media.

1 A selection of textures produced with different media.

❶ Black pencil and fine drawing pen
❷ Wax crayon on textured paper
❸ Watercolour over texture
❹ Watercolour and dry brush
❺ Pastel
❻ Ink
❼ Wax
❽ Paint and black wax pencil
❾ Charcoal pencil over texture
❿ Wire mesh texture
⓫ Black pencil and pastel

1 Right: Figures in reverse. Using the same pose in reverse can set off the design very effectively.

2 Textures are applied lightly to prevent the drawings becoming overworked.

3 Presentation: The completed figures are cut out and mounted against a contrasting background for clarity.

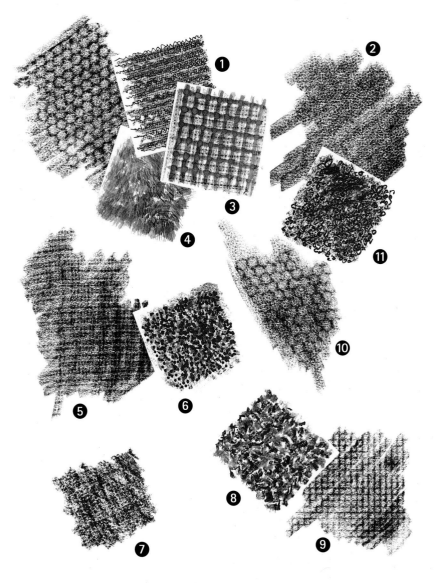

Markers

Oil Pastels

Textures

Coloured Pencils

1 Right: The line drawing is produced with a black Pentel pen.
2 Fine markers are used for the check shirt.
3 Areas of white are left on the trousers to suggest the movement of the figure.
4 Presentation: The figure is placed against a photograph to suggest the mood of the design and offset against a coloured panel.

Mounting Work on Card

- Cut out the illustration using a modelling knife, scalpel, guillotine or sharp pair of scissors.
- Apply adhesive to the back of the illustration.
- Position the illustration accurately on a piece of card and smooth it down. Always place a sheet of paper over the top of the drawing before smoothing it down.
- Spraymount adhesive comes in an aerosol can. It is clear and allows drawings to be repositioned. Only spray on one surface. Spraymount is most effective when used with very thin tissue papers.

- Select a variety of fabric samples and experiment reproducing their prints and textures with a selection of different media.
- Mix illustration techniques to achieve a wide range of effects.

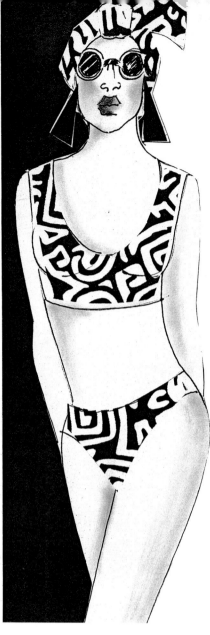

The Photocopier

The photocopier is an invaluable tool for the fashion illustrator and is used for black-and-white or colour work. It is particularly indispensible for collage work. The photocopier allows you to:

- Experiment on photocopies before adding colour and texture to original work.
- Transfer line drawings on to different coloured papers before

developing illustrations further.

- Photocopy drawings and photographs to transparent papers in black and white or colour. These can be used for presentation and display storyboards, project covers, tracing paper overlays and transparent film.
- Reduce fabric prints to the scale of your figures. Use tracing paper to trace the shapes of the garments,

apply to the photocopied print and cut out the new garment shape.

- Photocopy textured and patterned fabrics, reducing and enlarging the scale to match the drawings when using collage techniques.
- Copy photographs and other materials for background effects for storyboards.
- Take drawings down in size, allowing you to see the effect

when reduced for printing.

- Photocopy artwork for reference before sending originals off to a client, for competitions or for interviews.

- Photocopy reference work when researching and collecting material for sketch books and storyboards.

1 The sketches are cut out and spraymounted against a black panel to offset the silhouette of the figures.

2 The soft tone on the face and figure is applied with a cotton wool bud and grey pastel powder.

3 Fabric print is reduced to be used as part of a collage for the swimsuits on p74 and enlarged for the background effect on p75.

Watercolour

Watercolour paints are available in various forms. Tubes are ideal when large quantities of paint are needed. Palettes are more suitable when working on a small scale. Watercolour is a versatile medium allowing both fine detailed work and broad expressive statements. Choose the correct watercolour paper for the effect you require. There is a wide choice of both handmade and machine made papers. Rough textured papers allow a free use of washes and produce good textured effects. The smoother papers require a persistent application of paint as they do not hold it so firmly. A colour wash will cover an area with perfect flat colour.

- Work wet into wet to experiment with a softer look.
- Dry brush work is good for representing textures.
- Layer a wash against an edge to create a clearly defined line.

Experiment with different presentation ideas on the photocopier; enlarging, reducing and transferring sketches on to papers of different colours and textures.

- Practise photocopying patterns and weaves to the scale of your illustration.
- Always check whether the photocopier will take a greater thickness of paper without jamming.

1 Figures are sketched on to layout paper and photocopied on to tinted watercolour paper.
2 The sketches are coloured using watercolour washes.
3 Presentation: The figures are cut out and placed against photographs that have been enlarged on the photocopier.

1 Fabric prints are photocopied and taken down to scale and then applied to sketches and background for collage effects.

• Enlarge prints for backgrounds and reduce for figures.

• Offset prints against a contrasting background.

• Show details of seams, collars and folds with a white line in pencil, pen and ink or paint, or by cutting out sections in the paper.

• Cropping figures can be very effective for emphasizing a particular aspect of the illustration in the presentation.

The Airbrush

The number of types of airbrush on the market is considerable but divide into two basic kinds: single action and double action. With the single action lever mechanism, the density of the spray is varied by altering the distance between the brush and the surface of the paper. The more sophisticated double action lever airbrush allows greater control and variety. The lever controls both the air and the colour. The more you press down on the lever, the more the air is released; the more you pull back the lever, the more paint is released into the airstream. The compressed air can be supplied by aerosol cans or by an electric compressor. The latter is expensive but the most efficient. The airbrush must be kept clean to ensure correct functioning. The medium to use with an airbrush is one that will give a fine spray: ink, watercolour, gouache and acrylic paint are all suitable.

- Experiment with the airbrush to create faultless flat tones, graded tones and blended effects.

- Practise brush ruling, sliding the airbrush along an angled straight edge and curved shapes.
- Choose a surface without too much texture as this will affect the quality of tone.
- Make sure the medium used in the airbrush has been properly diluted. If this has not been done, the airbrush spray will give a

grainy and stippled effect to the artwork, and may also cause the nozzel to clog.

- To avoid clogging, the paint reservoir should be cleaned with each change of colour by spraying water or a solvent cleaner through the fluid chamber.

1 The line drawing is covered with masking film.
2 Sections of film are cut away.

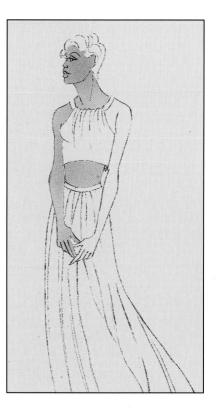

3 Right: After the illustration has been sprayed, it is completed with a photograph and an airbrush background.

Masking Work

The use of masking film is an essential technique when working with the airbrush.

- Cover the illustration with an adhesive masking film and expose sections of the image by cutting out areas with a very sharp scalpel. Do not cut too deep and score the illustration under the film.
- Remove a section of the mask, spray the revealed area and allow it to dry.
- Replace the section of mask over the sprayed illustration, and repeat the process for other areas.
- When the illlustration is complete, peel all the film away.
- Try using liquid masking to cover irregular or small and complicated areas. It is applied with a brush and may be peeled away easily once the area has dried.

The airbrush requires practice to acquire advanced skills, but many effects may be produced using simple methods of presentation.

- Practise with the airbrush to achieve line values, curves and tonal shading.
- Try spraying through lace, net or stencils.
- Attach different nozzels to the airbrush to achieve a splattered effect, fine lines or a broad spray.

1 Left: A selection of graduated airbrush effects used as backgrounds to fashion illustrations.

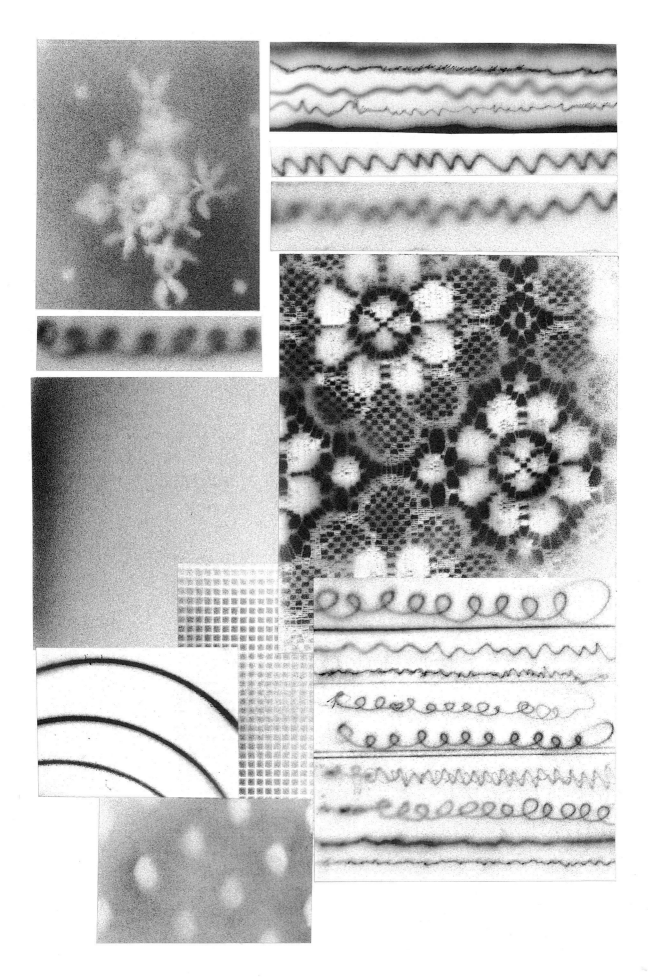

Collage

1 The figures are cut out of a tan coloured pastel paper.
2 Black card is used for the hair shapes.
3 The bracelets are represented with pieces of bronze card.
4 Fabric is photocopied and reduced to the scale of the drawings for the swimwear.
5 Presentation: The figures are spraymounted to a blue presentation board, with torn blue tissue paper representing the sea.

Collage is the use of cut and torn paper of neat or abstract shapes and paper is often combined with photographs and fabrics. Collage work may vary from a very free style of applying the pieces to a more controlled approach, depending on the purpose of the work and the effect you wish to achieve. This technique is often used when creating storyboards for research, fashion forecasting or textile promotion.

- Experiment with collage using papers, fabric, magazine cuttings and photographs.
- Apply objects on the surface of the artwork for a three-dimensional effect.
- Collect a selection of papers in different colours, patterns and textures to use in collage.

1 The figure is drawn with a Pentel Sign pen, using a bold, clear line.
2 Papers are applied to sections of the drawing, leaving areas of white to emphasize the shapes.
3 Patterned fabric is reduced on the photocopier for the background and trousers.
4 Tissue papers are used for the jumper and boots, and thin black card for the hair.

Theatre Costume Illustration

Designing costume for the stage, screen or television is a separate discipline of fashion design and the approach to fashion graphics tends to be very different. The design drawings have to depict the characters of the production as well as their garments and statements are often over-emphasized to make an impact. It is important to research costume and accessories from different periods as this has to be reflected in the costume design.

1 Designs for J.B. Priestley's 'Laburnum Grove' by Stephen West.

2 The illustrations use textured acrylic for the background and fine pencil applied to gouache for the costume design.

Venice carnival costume designs by
Val Fisher, programme director, BA
Costume for the Screen and Stage,
Bournemouth College of Art and
Design, interpreted by first year
BA students.

1 Male and female fancy dress
inspired by a Pietro Longhi
painting. Drawings in acrylic,
costumes in silk faille.

2 Drawing in oil pastel with
acrylic overlaid and then
scraped away to achieve the
striped effect. The costume is
made up in gold and cream
ribbon and striped organza and
trimmed with violet ribbon.

1 Left: Mixed media and glitter glue.

2 Below: Mixed media, including watercolour, gouache, pencil, crayon, pastels and glitter glue.

Designs for the ballet, 'The
Sleeping Beauty'.

1 Carabosse the evil fairy
  by Corinna Vincent
  (HND2 Costume)

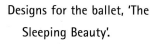

Theatre costume is designed to be
seen on the stage or screen with
lighting and scenery effects, often
from a distance, therefore the
statements must be bold and over-
emphasized to be seen.
Alternatively, close up shots are
sometimes needed, so very detailed
and accurate work can be required.
Costume design drawings vary from
very free stylized sketches to a
more illustrative graphic technique.
This section illustrates examples of
work produced by students and
professional designers for a
selection of productions. The
design sketches use a variety of
techniques and media to produce a
strong presentation. Fabrics,
decorative surfaces and textures are
all depicted and samples of fabrics
and trimmings are attached to the
design sheets and notes added
when extra information is required.

A costume designer would work
with the director together with the
production team, co-ordinating
with the costume workroom staff,
make-up and hairdressers, set and
lighting designers and other
members of the production team.

2 Carobosse's attendant by
  Caroline Wills (HND2
  Costume)

MR
PETER
RAFFAN
AS
CAPTAIN
FLASH

1 Design for Captain Flash from Garrick`s 'Miss in her teens' by Stephen West.

2 The illustration uses gouache, acrylics and pen.

Art Materials

A large selection of art materials is available. New items are constantly introduced, so offering you the opportunity to develop new techniques. Be aware of new products and experiment with them. Many art materials are available as single items as well as a complete range of colours. Initially, it is advisable to purchase a small selection of colours to discover how you relate to the medium. Often special papers, fixatives and solvents will be needed to achieve the required effects.

Fashion boards
High quality thick board that will take charcoal, crayon, gouache, tempera and watercolour paints.

Watercolour boards
Saunders Water Colour Boards prepared from a mouldmade paper. The paper has an even surface.

Bristol board
The board has a high rag content with a fine white surface. Ideal for pen and ink work.

Pasteboard
An inexpensive white board for paste-up and general studio use.

Illustration boards
A board with a smooth surface which will take ink, crayon, pencil, wash or colour. Produced in different sizes.

Cartridge paper
White paper with a finely grained surface suitable for pencil, crayon and colour. This paper is made in different thicknesses and qualities.

Coloured cartridge paper
The surface has a slight texture. Suitable for colour work. Will take watercolour and pastels.

Layout pads
White layout detail paper with a surface ideal for ink and pencil. Available in different sizes.

Ingres paper
The surface of this paper is ideal for pastel and tempera work. Available in a good selection of colours.

Coloured tissue papers
Unglazed tissue paper, available in a large range of colours, is used in studios to produce inexpensive colour effects. The paper can be stuck to board or paper surfaces with cow gum or adhesive spray.

Tracing paper and pads
Obtainable in sheets of different sizes or pads.

Herculene tracing film
Polyester film of good quality. Will take pencil and ink, ideal for photocopying and also colour separation work. May also be used for the protection of work.

Permatrace
Film with an excellent drawing surface for ink and pencil. This film is virtually indestructible.

Tracing cloth
Good quality tracing cloth for work that must withstand considerable handling and wear.

Detail paper
A white paper with a high degree of transparency. Suitable when working from original roughs.

Pencils

A large selection of pencils is obtainable; the type of pencil used depends on the effect required.

Pencils (wood cased)
The degree of hardness is printed on each pencil:
6B is very soft, 9H very hard
F and HB medium
EX is extremely soft

Stabilo pencils
This pencil will write on any surface: film, glossy photographs, metals, etc.

Charcoal pencils
Give the same effect as pure charcoal sticks. Made in hard, medium or soft qualities.

Carbon pencils
This pencil will produce a dull matt finish.

Black pencils
Heavy extra large leads for bold drawings in matt jet black.

Coloured pencils
A large variety of makes is available with a good range of colours.

Watercolour pencils
Soft water soluble pencils. Use dry or wash over with a brush to achieve watercolour effects.

Chinagraph
This wax-based pencil is impervious to water and dampness, though it can be removed with a dry cloth.

Pens

A large selection of pens is available; listed are some chosen for the different effects they achieve.

Rapidograph pens
Technical pens that provide a means of drawing without the need for constant refilling. The drawing point may be replaced with different sizes.

Osmiroid fountain pens
A pen for lettering and script writing, available in a large range of interchangeable screw-in nibs. Not suitable for use with Indian ink.

Technos drawing pen
The Pelikan Technos is a cartridge-filled drawing pen. Pen points are designed for different jobs, e.g. ruling, stencilling, and free hand. Many interchangeable points are available.

Marker pens
Large range of colours available. Quick drying. Chisel tip allows precise control of line from fine detail work to broad strokes. Obtainable with interchangable nibs in one barrel.

Osmiroid Sketch fountain pen
A very versatile sketching pen which provides a wide variety of line thickness from bold to a fine outline. This pen is fitted with a reservoir to maintain a constant ink flow. Indian ink should not be used.

Pen holders
Many very simple wood or plastic pen holders with nibs are obtainable at a small cost.

Inks
Watercolour inks can be mixed with one another or diluted with water. A large range of colours is available. Very effective when used with the airbrush.

Acrylic colours
Extremely versatile, can be used with a variety of techniques. Easily diluted with water, but waterproof when dry.

A large selection of paints of varying qualities are manufactured:
Watercolours
Designer colours
Coloured designer inks
Tubes of oil paint.

Pastels

Pastels vary depending on the quality.

Coloured inks
A large selection of coloured inks are available, some of which are waterproof.

Brushes
Brushes are made in many sizes and qualities (sable, hog and squirrel hair).

Transparent acetate sheet
Cellulose acetate film. Suitable for covering art work and presentation.

Presentation books
Fitted with clear acetate pockets, ideal for the presentation of work.

Portfolios
Strong durable portfolios in different sizes for storing art work.

Leathercloth portfolios
Ideal for the protection and carrying of art work. Fitted with handle, two fasteners and a centre lock and key. Made in different sizes.

Stanley knife
A craft knife with replaceable blades, ideal for cutting thick paper, heavy card, plastics, etc.

Swivel-head knife
Cuts irregular curves, may be locked for straight lines.

Cutting mats
Non-slip mats that provide a safe surface for all cutting jobs. Are printed with a grid. Special self-healing surface.

Double-sided adhesive tape
Suitable for quick mounting. Adhesive on both sides.

Protective sprays
Protects art work against damage. Obtainable in gloss or matt.

Adhesive in aerosol cans
Spray adhesive that is colourless and water repellent. Will stick cloth, board, paper.

Spraymount
Remount creative adhesive allows you to lift and remount work without respraying. Allows experimentation with positioning of visuals prior to finished artwork.

Cow gum
Transparent rubber solution suitable for pasting work up. Sold in tins or tubes.

Copydex
Very strong latex adhesive, may be used with paper and fabric.

Gum eraser or paper cleaner
A soft pliable eraser gum. Suitable for cleaning art work. Will not damage the surface of the paper.

Kneaded eraser
A putty rubber that can be moulded to the shape required.

Staedtler Mars plastic
For use on drafting film, tracing cloth or paper.

Soft eraser
A white soft eraser for soft lead.

Masking tape
Tape that seals with a light pressure. Has a water-repellent back.

Drafting tape
A very thin, adhesive crepe paper tape designed to hold film or paper to drawing boards. It can be removed without damage.

Light box
A box with a glass top containing a light, used for tracing.

Transpaseal
Flexible sheet of thin transparent plastic coated with a pressure-sensitive adhesive, obtainable in clear gloss or matt finish. Suitable for covering art work.

Airbrush
The airbrush provides perfectly even tones, graded tints and soft lines, and also blends colours. Operated by a motor compressor or compressed air propellant aerosols.

Book List

Fashion Illustration

Barnes, Colin, *Fashion Illustration*, Macdonald, 1988

Drake, Nicholas, *Fashion Illustration Today*, Thames & Hudson, 1987

Illustrator's Figure Reference Manual, Bloomsbury Publishing Ltd, 1987

Ireland, Patrick John, *Encyclopedia of Fashion Details*, Batsford, 1996

Ireland, Patrick John, *Fashion Design Drawing and Illustration*, Batsford, 1982

Ireland, Patrick John, *Introduction to Fashion Design*, Batsford, 1996

Kumager, Kojiro, *Fashion Illustrations*, Graphic-Sha, 1988

Parker, William, *Fashion Drawing in Vogue*, Thames & Hudson, 1983

Yajima, Isao, *Figure Drawing for Fashion*, Graphic-Sha, 1990

Yajima, Isao, *Mode Drawing*, Graphic-Sha, 1989

Figure Drawing

Croney, John, *Drawing Figure Movement*, Batsford, 1983

Everett, Felicity, *Fashion Design*, Usborne, 1987

Gordon, Louise, *Anatomy and Figure Drawing*, Batsford, 1996

Loomis, Andrew, *Figure Drawing for all it's Worth*, Viking Press, 1971

Smith, Stan and Wheeler, Linda, *Drawing and Painting the Figure*, Phaidon, 1983

Graphics

The Artist's Manual, *Painting and Drawing Materials and Techniques*, Harper Collins, 1995

Cuthbert, Rosalind, *The Pastel Painter's Pocket Palette*, Batsford

Dalley, Terence (Consultant Editor), *The Complete Guide to Illustration and Design Techniques and Materials*, Phaidon, 1980

Hicks, Roger W., *The Airbrushing Book*, produced in association with Aztek Broadcast Books

Laing, J and Davis R.S., *Graphic Tools and Techniques*, Blandford Press, 1986

Lewis, Brian, *An Introduction to Illustration*, The Apple Press, 1987

Sidaway, Ian, *The Acrylic Painter's Pocket Palette*, Batsford, 1994

Smith, Ray, *The Artist Handbook*, Dorling Kindersley

Strother, Jane, *The Coloured Pencil Artist Pocket Palette*, Batsford

Welling, Richard, *Drawing with Markers*, Pitman, 1974

History of Fashion

Antonio, *Three Decades of Fashion Illustration*, Thames & Hudson, 1995

Blum, Stella, *Designs by Erté*, Dover Publications, New York, 1976

Boucher, Francis, *A History of Costume in the West*, Thames & Hudson, 1966

Davenport, Millia, *The Book of Costume*, Crown, New York, 1976

Ewing, Elizabeth and Mackrell, Alice, *History of Twentieth Century Fashion*, Batsford, New Edition, 1992

Milbank, Caroline Reynolds, *Couture - The Great Fashion Designers*, Thames & Hudson, 1985

Murray, Maggie Pexton, *Changing Styles in Fashion*, Fairchild Publications, New York, 1989

O'Hara, Georgina, *The Encyclopaedia of Fashion*, Thames & Hudson, 1986

Peacock, John, *The Chronicle of Western Costume*, Thames & Hudson, 1991

Stegemeyer, Anne, *Who's Who in Fashion*, Fairchild, 1988

Tilke, Max, *Costume Patterns and Design*, Magna Books, 1990

Index